D1624646

First published in 1992
by Thomas Nelson Publishers, Nashville,
Tennessee, and distributed in Canada by
Lawson Falle, Ltd., Cambridge, Ontario.

Copyright © 1992 Oyster Books Ltd

10 9 8 7 6 5 4 3 2 1

Library of Congress Cataloging
in Publication Data is available.

Library of Congress Card
92-080772

ISBN 0-8407-6868-0

Printed in Italy

Text retold by Tim and Jenny Wood

Design by Pinpoint Design Ltd

JONAH
AND THE
BIG FISH

THOMAS NELSON PUBLISHERS

NASHVILLE

From time to time God chose certain people to carry special messages for Him. One of the people He chose was an Israelite called Jonah.

God wanted Jonah to carry a message to the city of Nineveh in the land of Assyria.

"Jonah," said God. "The people of Nineveh are very wicked. You must go there and tell them to change, or I will destroy the city."

Jonah was not happy about going to Nineveh, because the Assyrians were the enemies of the Israelites. He knew that they were very mean.

"Why should I warn the people of Nineveh?" thought Jonah, as he packed for the trip. "They deserve to be punished for their wickedness."

So Jonah decided to disobey God. He set out on his trip, but he went in the opposite direction. He went to Joppa and found a ship which was going to Tarshish in Spain. Tarshish was about as far away from Nineveh as Jonah could get.

Jonah went on board the ship and paid his fare. Then he lay down and went to sleep, relieved that he would not have to go to Nineveh.

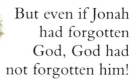

But even if Jonah had forgotten God, God had not forgotten him! Soon after the ship set sail, a terrible storm started. The wind roared and howled, whipping up the water into huge waves. The ship was tossed like a cork on the raging sea, and the sailors were afraid that the ship would sink. They threw the cargo overboard to make the ship lighter and cried out to all their gods to help them.

Jonah was so tired that he managed to sleep through all the commotion. But after a while the captain came to wake him.

"Get up!" the captain ordered. "We are all going to be drowned. You'd better start praying."

Jonah got up and went on deck.

The sailors were clinging to the mast to keep from being washed overboard.

"I've never seen a storm like this," one of them shouted above the roar of the wind.

"The gods must be angry with someone," another sailor yelled.

"If only we knew who it was," said a third.

Jonah felt very guilty.

"It's my fault," he confessed, "my God gave me a job to do, and I ran away. He made the earth and the sea, and I think He must have sent this storm because I disobeyed Him."

This news made
the sailors even
more afraid.
"What can
we do to make
this storm stop?" they asked.

"You must throw me
overboard!" Jonah bravely replied.
He realized now that God would
not allow him to squirm out of
the job he had been given, and
that his plan was the only way
to stop the storm.

The sailors were kind men.
They did not want Jonah to
drown. But the storm was getting
worse every moment, and they
did not know what to do.

The sailors got out the oars and tried to row, but the wind was too strong.

"Jonah's God must be very powerful," they said. "The storm is getting fiercer. Unless we do as Jonah says, the ship will be wrecked and we'll all drown. We must get rid of Jonah, it's our only hope."

So the sailors picked up Jonah and threw him into the raging sea.

Immediately, the storm died down and the sea became calm. The sailors were amazed.

"Jonah's God is the only true god," they said. "We will believe in Him from now on."

The captain and the sailors knelt on the deck and prayed. But this time they spoke to God and thanked Him for saving them all.

Meanwhile, Jonah floated away from the ship. He was very frightened because he was sure he would drown.

"I am miles from land," he thought, miserably. "How stupid I was to think that I could disobey God."

He soon became tired and cold. Seaweed stuck to his head and arms. Jonah knew he could not swim much further. He was going to drown. Desperately he began to pray.

"Help me, God!" he shouted, choking on a mouthful of salt water.

God heard Jonah's prayer.
He sent help to Jonah in a most
unusual way. A gigantic fish

swam under the drowning man,
opened its mouth and swallowed
him whole!

Jonah was safe, but he was still very frightened. It was dark, smelly and cold inside the fish. He had plenty of time to think about what had happened. He realized that he had been very stupid to run away. He also knew that, although he had been thrown into the sea, God had saved him. Jonah made up his mind that he would go to Nineveh after all.

Three days later, the great fish spit Jonah out onto a beach.

"Now, Jonah," said God, "I've given you a second chance. Go to Nineveh and give the people my message."

This time Jonah did as he was told. He went to Nineveh and gave the people God's message. The people not only listened to Jonah, they also believed him.

They decided to show God how sorry they were. All the people, even the king himself, took off their rich clothes, put on rags and rubbed ashes on their faces. God saw what they did and forgave them for all their wickedness.

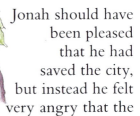

Jonah should have been pleased that he had saved the city, but instead he felt very angry that the wicked people of Nineveh had not been punished. He went outside the walls, sat under a shady plant and sulked. But God had one final lesson for him. He made the plant which kept Jonah cool, droop and die. Without shade, Jonah began to feel hot and ill.

"You're sorry that I destroyed the plant, aren't you?" said God. "Don't you think that I would have been even sorrier to destroy a great city and thousands of helpless people? Be happy that I saved them."

And for the first time during his long adventure, Jonah really was happy.

Jonah 1:1–4:11